The Booby Trap

Written by John Lockyer
Illustrated by John Bennett

Simon and Nat lay on the ground under a sprawling tree. It was too hot for a kickabout. Suddenly, Simon's sister, Rachel, ran towards them from the end of the park.

"My kite," she shouted. "It's stuck in the big oak tree."

The boys wandered over to the tree. Simon grabbed the string and tugged, but the kite wouldn't budge.

"We'll have to climb up," he said.

They reached the kite easily. Just as they were pulling the kite free, Nat hissed and pressed a finger to his lips. He pointed to a house next to the park. A ladder leaned against a wall below an upstairs window. They could see a man inside sweeping things from the shelves into an open bag.

The boys climbed down quietly. They told Rachel about the burglar.

"Hey," she said. "I'll bet that motorbike we saw in the bushes was his."

"His bag is almost full," Simon went on. "But there's no time to call the police. We have to stop him."

Nat frowned. "How? He could be dangerous."

Simon stared at the garden shed and smiled. "We'll booby-trap him! There'll be heaps of stuff to use in that shed. But first we need a plan. Let's go into the shed, grab whatever we can, and set the traps. Okay?"

He didn't wait for any questions. He was already crawling through the garden.

5

The burglar slipped out of the window. He gripped the ladder, keeping his face towards the house, and stepped down slowly.

When he was almost at the bottom, he suddenly yelled and shook his hand. The bag slipped from his shoulder and threw him off balance. Still shaking his hand, he looked at the ladder. There were pins stuck to it with putty.

Twisting on the ladder, he stared around the yard. When he was sure there was no one there, he stepped to the ground and hurried along the path.

Suddenly the burglar stumbled and tripped over. Leaping to his feet, he beat the bushes beside the path. But again, there was no one there.

The burglar ripped the hidden tripwire off the trees, picked up his bag and walked on, making sure he kept his eyes down. He didn't see the plastic bag whizzing through the air. It hit him on the chest, burst and splattered him with bright yellow paint.

He stumbled to the ground and grabbed handfuls of grass to wipe the sticky mess off his clothes. Again, he looked around.

"I know you're here somewhere," he muttered wildly. "If I get my hands on you!"

But he knew he had to keep moving.

The burglar picked up the bag again and walked on, stopping often to scan the garden. When he reached the back gate, he grabbed the latch and pulled. The gate was jammed.

He let the latch go and waited but nothing happened. He looked all around the latch but there were no hidden wires.

He muttered to himself, then climbed onto the wooden fence beside the gate. When he reached the top rail, he swung a leg over and rested a moment. Then he found he couldn't move. He wriggled and jiggled about, trying to free himself, but he was stuck fast. He put both hands on the rail and felt something wet and sticky.

Superglue!

The burglar jammed his feet on the rail and pushed. His pants ripped, but he didn't stop. He kept pushing until he had torn himself free. Then he jumped to the ground and ran for his motorbike.

Simon, Nat and Rachel ducked behind some bushes. They tried to muffle their laughs when they saw his red, polka-dot underpants through the hole in his jeans.

"Watch this," said Rachel.

The burglar had his bike out of the bushes. He jumped on the kick-start. The engine groaned.

He jumped again. The engine coughed and rumbled, then a lemon shot out of the exhaust pipe and blasted into a nearby garden. Glass smashed and someone shrieked. A man looked over the hedge, saw the burglar and grabbed his phone.

The bike started and the burglar sped between
two trees. He didn't see the thin rope
stretched across the gap. The rope hit
him across the chest and knocked
him to the ground.

Simon, Nat and Rachel pounced on the bag of stolen goods. The burglar staggered towards them. "So it's you!" he shouted. "Just you wait!"

"Hey!" shouted the man with the phone, who had come into the park.

The burglar turned and ran.

"He's getting away!" Simon shouted.

"He won't get far," said the man.

At the main park gates, the children were just in time to see two police officers push the burglar into a police car.

Simon laughed. "I know a great headline for tomorrow's newspaper. 'Purglar comes to a sticky end'."

The Booby Trap is a Narrative.

A narrative has an introduction It tells . . .

- who the story is about (the characters)
- where the story happened
- when the story happened.

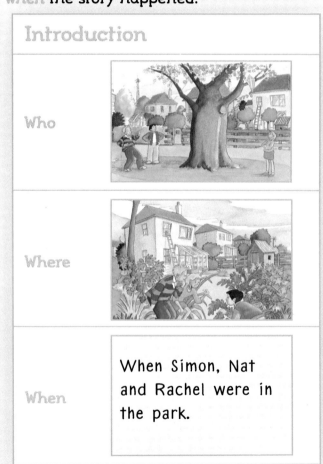

Introduction	
Who	
Where	
When	When Simon, Nat and Rachel were in the park.

A narrative has a problem and a solution

Problem

Solution

Guide Notes

Title: The Booby Trap
Stage: Fluency

Text Form: Narrative
Approach: Guided Reading
Processes: Thinking Critically, Exploring Language, Processing Information
Written and Visual Focus: Speech Bubbles

THINKING CRITICALLY
(sample questions)
- What do you think this story could be about? Look at the title and discuss.
- Look at the cover. What is a booby trap? What do you think the children are doing?
- Look at pages 2 and 3. What do you think the man in the house is doing?
- Look at pages 4 and 5. Do you think the children should have called the police? How do you think they could booby-trap the burglar?
- Look at pages 8 and 9. Why do you think the burglar had to keep moving?
- Look at pages 14 and 15. Do you think it was a good idea for the children to booby-trap the burglar?
- Look at pages 16 and 17. What does the headline "Burglar comes to a sticky end" mean?

EXPLORING LANGUAGE

Terminology
Spread, author and illustrator credits, imprint information, ISBN number

Vocabulary
Clarify: booby trap, burglar, exhaust pipe, stolen goods
Adjectives: *polka-dot* underpants, *sprawling* tree, *hidden* tripwire
Pronouns: them, my, he, they, his, he
Adverbs: climbed down *quietly*; stepped down *slowly*
Focus the students' attention on **homonyms**, **antonyms** and **synonyms** if appropriate.